DATE DUE

First Facts®

The Solar System

The Milky Way

by Steve Kortenkamp

Consultant:
James Gerard
Aerospace Education Specialist, NASA
Kennedy Space Center, Florida

Capstone press®

Mankato, Minnesota

First Facts is published by Capstone Press,
151 Good Counsel Drive, P.O. Box 669, Mankato, Minnesota 56002.
www.capstonepress.com

Library of Congress Cataloging-in-Publication Data
Kortenkamp, Steve.
    The Milky Way / by Steve Kortenkamp.
    p. cm.—(First facts. The Solar system)
    Summary: "Describes our galaxy, the Milky Way, including its size, shape, and movement
through the universe"—Provided by publisher.
    Includes bibliographical references and index.
    ISBN-13: 978-1-4296-0061-3 (hardcover)
    ISBN-10: 1-4296-0061-6 (hardcover)
    1. Milky Way—Juvenile literature. I. Title. II. Series.
QB857.7.K67 2008
523.1′13—dc22   2006100044

Editorial Credits
Jennifer Besel, editor; Juliette Peters, set designer; Patrick Dentinger, book designer; Jo Miller,
    photo researcher

Photo Credits
Comstock Images, 19
Getty Images Inc./Hulton Archive, 16
iStockphoto/Shaun Lowe, 1
NASA, 8–9; ESA, K. Sahu (STScl) and the SWEEPS science team, 21; The Hubble Heritage Team
    and A. Riess (STScl), 15; The Hubble Heritage Team (AURA/STScI/NASA), 7; The Hubble
    Heritage Team, STScl, AURA, 20; R. Hurt (SSC), JPL-Caltech, 10–11
NSSDC, 12
Peter Arnold, Inc./Astrofoto, cover
Shutterstock/Shawn Talbot, 4–5

1 2 3 4 5 6 12 11 10 09 08 07

Table of Contents

Seeing the Milky Way

A faint band of light stretches across the night sky. A long time ago, people thought this fuzzy white path looked like milk. They named it the Milky Way.

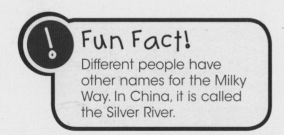

Fun Fact!
Different people have other names for the Milky Way. In China, it is called the Silver River.

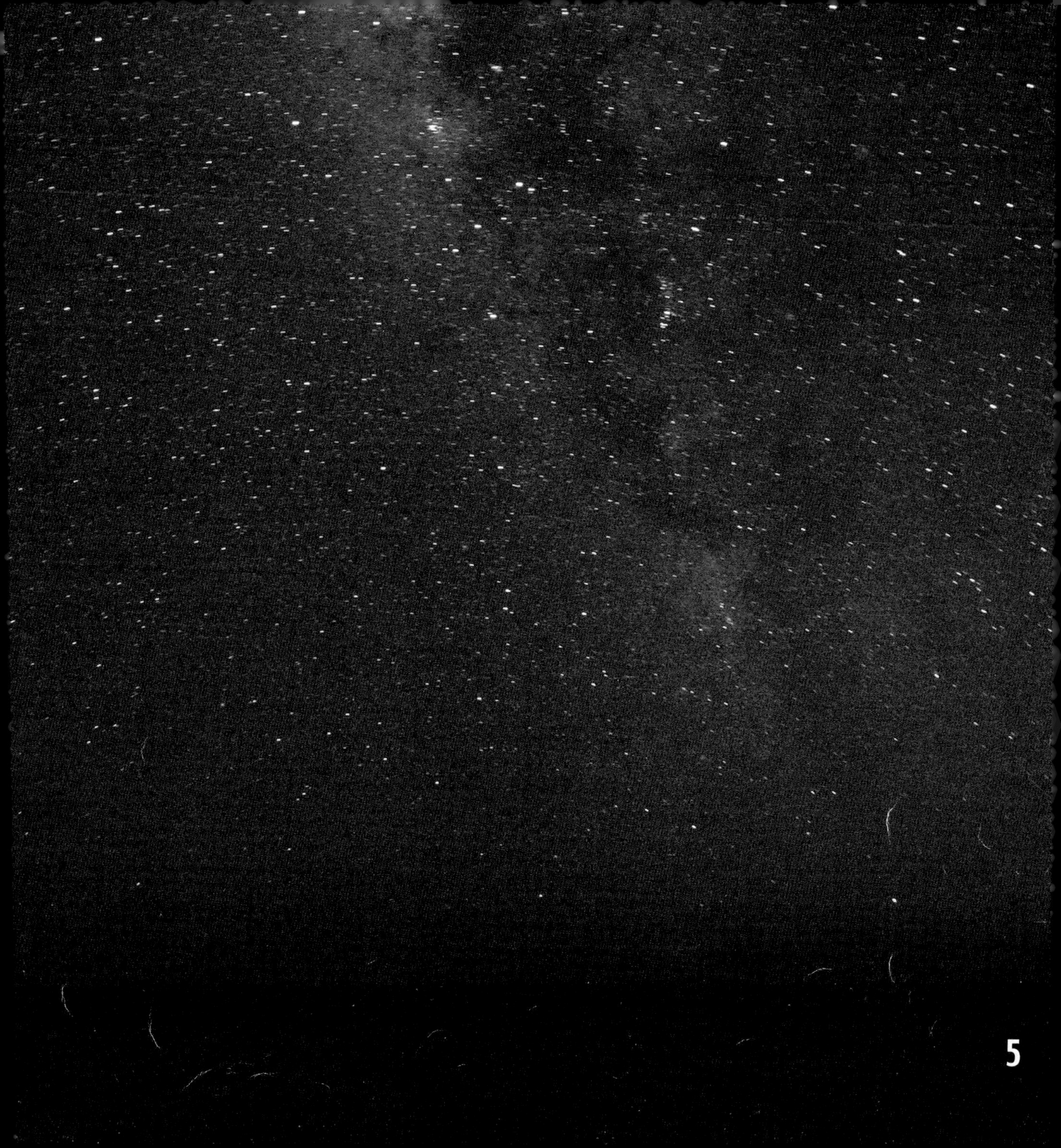

What Is the Milky Way?

Today, we know that the Milky Way is a huge group of stars called a **galaxy**. Our Sun is only one of the billions and billions of stars in the Milky Way.

The solar system we call home is a very tiny part of the Milky Way. Other stars in our galaxy have planets moving around them too.

! Fun Fact!
The Milky Way isn't the only galaxy. There are billions of other galaxies.

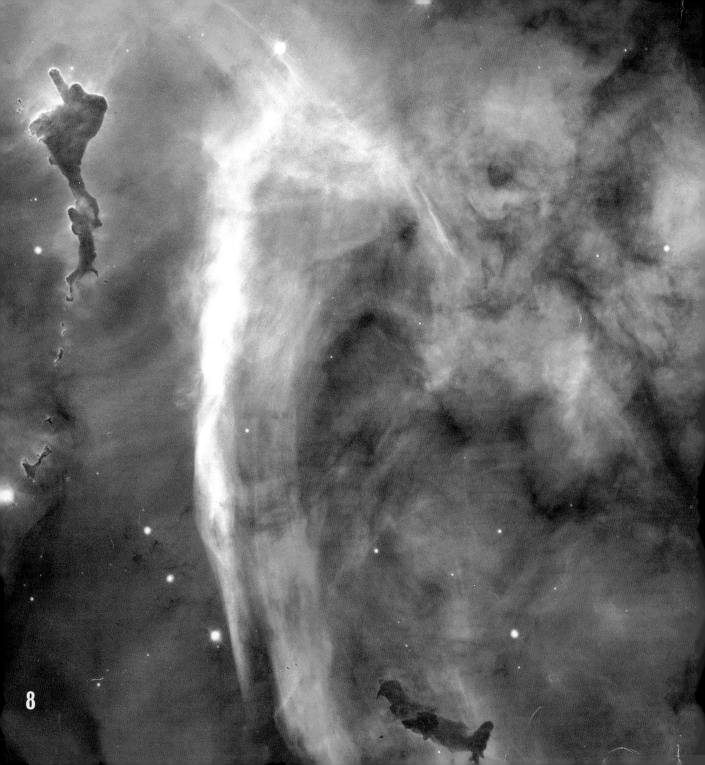

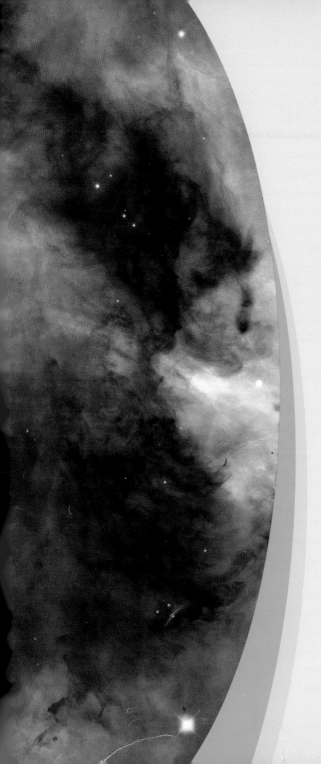

Our galaxy isn't made up of just stars and planets. The Milky Way also has giant clouds of gas and dust. **Gravity** from all the gas, dust, and stars holds the galaxy together.

! **Fun Fact!**
One of the Milky Way's gas clouds is shaped like a horse's head.

The Milky Way's Shape

The Milky Way is a spiral galaxy. It has long arms of dust and stars. These arms spread out in a circle that looks like a pinwheel. The middle of the circle is shaped like a ball. Many, many stars are crowded in that space.

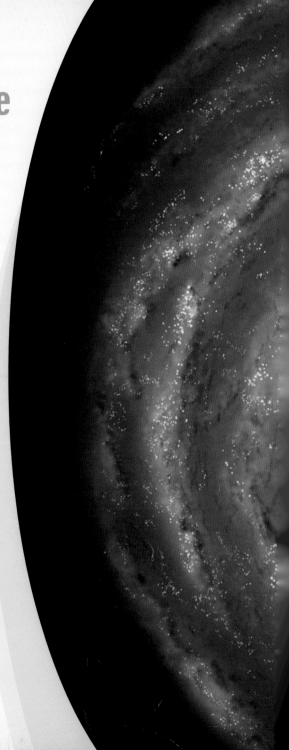

11

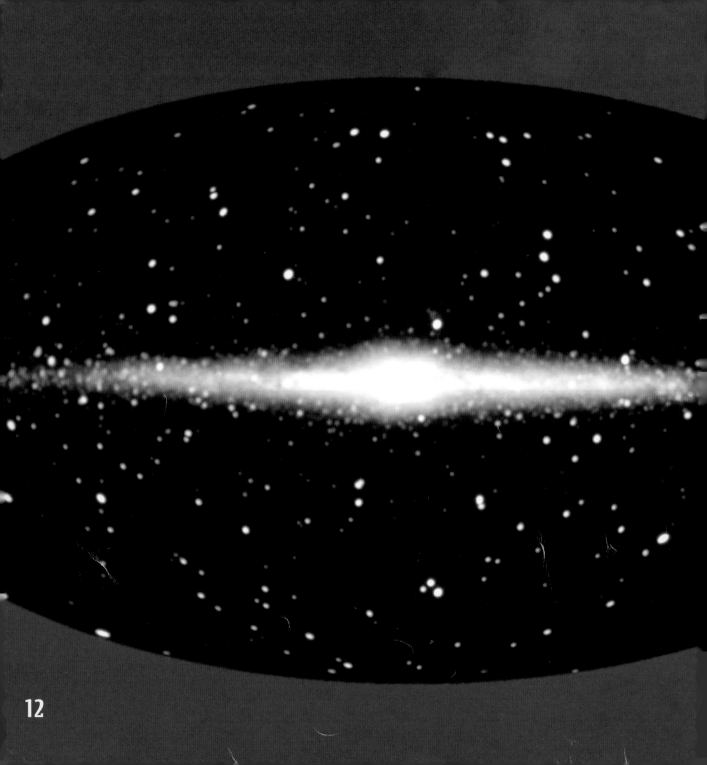

The Size of Our Galaxy

Scientists use the speed of light to measure really long distances. Light travels almost six trillion miles (10 trillion kilometers) in one year. Scientists call that distance a light-year.

The Milky Way galaxy is 100,000 light-years from edge to edge. If a **spacecraft** could travel at the speed of light, it would take 100,000 years to cross the galaxy.

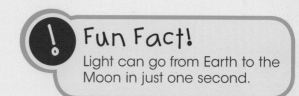

Fun Fact!
Light can go from Earth to the Moon in just one second.

Our Place in the Galaxy

The Sun and planets of our solar system live in a small spiral arm named Orion. Orion is about halfway out from the center of the Milky Way.

Our Sun and all the other stars **orbit** around the center of the Milky Way. It takes our Sun 250 million years to go just once around the galaxy.

our solar system

Studying the Milky Way

In 1609, the **astronomer** Galileo Galilei turned his telescope to the sky. He saw that the Milky Way was made up of billions of stars. Since that time, astronomers have studied the Milky Way. They are trying to answer questions about our galaxy. How did the stars form? Are there other planets like Earth out there?

To answer their questions, astronomers use **radio telescopes**. These telescopes let astronomers see inside the Milky Way's gas clouds. They have learned that new stars are born inside these dark clouds. They hope that other discoveries like this will help solve the mysteries of the galaxy.

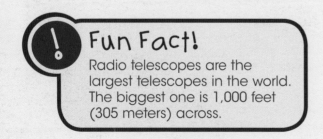

Fun Fact!

Radio telescopes are the largest telescopes in the world. The biggest one is 1,000 feet (305 meters) across.

Amazing but True!

Every once in a while, two galaxies crash into each other and form one galaxy. Right now, the Milky Way and another galaxy called Andromeda are moving toward each other. One day, these galaxies will collide. But don't worry, it won't happen for another 3 billion years!

Think Big!

Our galaxy has billions of stars. Astronomers have discovered new planets circling some of these stars. They are trying to find out if these planets could have life on them. One thing astronomers look for is water. What else do you think they should look for to see if another planet in our galaxy could have life?

The green circles mark distant stars with planets.

Glossary

astronomer (uh-STRON-uh-mur)—a scientist who studies stars, planets, and other objects in space

galaxy (GAL-uhk-see)—a large group of stars and planets

gravity (GRAV-uh-tee)—a force that pulls objects together

orbit (OR-bit)—to circle another object in space

radio telescope (RAY-dee-oh TEL-uh-skope)—an instrument that collects radio waves put out by objects in space; the waves are processed by computers to make a picture of where they came from.

spacecraft (SPAYSS-kraft)—a vehicle that travels in space

Read More

Asimov, Isaac. *The Milky Way and Other Galaxies.* Isaac Asimov's 21st Century Library of the Universe. Near and Far. Milwaukee: Gareth Stevens, 2005.

Elish, Dan. *Galaxies.* Kaleidoscope. New York: Marshall Cavendish Benchmark, 2007.

Rau, Dana Meachen. *The Milky Way and Other Galaxies.* Our Solar System. Minneapolis: Compass Point Books, 2005.

Internet Sites

FactHound offers a safe, fun way to find Internet sites related to this book. All of the sites on FactHound have been researched by our staff.

Here's how:

1. Visit *www.facthound.com*
2. Choose your grade level.
3. Type in this book ID **1429600616** for age-appropriate sites. You may also browse subjects by clicking on letters, or by clicking on pictures and words.
4. Click on the **Fetch It** button.

Facthound will fetch the best sites for you!

Index